A·L·I·V·E

FOR EVERMORE

Worship Resources
for
Lent and Easter

C.S.S. Publishing Co., Inc.

Lima, Ohio

ALIVE FOR EVERMORE: WORSHIP RESOURCES FOR LENT AND EASTER

ACKNOWLEDGEMENTS

Ash Wednesday service designed by Mary Lou Grossman, C.S.S. Publishing Co., Lima, Ohio © 1982; Palm Sunday service, C.S.S. Publishing Co., Lima, Ohio, © 1975; Maundy Thursday service, C.S.S. Publishing Co., Lima, Ohio, © 1988; Good Friday service (1), designed by Mary Lou Grossman, C.S.S. Publishing Co., Lima, Ohio © 1980; Good Friday service (2), C.S.S. Publishing Co., Lima, Ohio, © 1981; Easter Sunrise service, designed by Mary Lou Grossman, C.S.S. Publishing Co., Lima, Ohio, © 1981; Easter Morning service, C.S.S. Publishing Co., Lima, Ohio, © 1981.

9029 / ISBN 1-55673-212-0

Table of Contents

3

Service for Ash Wednesday

Light Service — Lighting of the Candles

Minister: Christ our Light.

People: Praise to you, Lord Christ.

Hymn (In honor of the light)

Minister: The Lord be with you.

People: And also with you.

Minister: Let us give thanks and praise to the Lord our God.

People: It is right that we should do so.

Minister: All praise and thanks we give to you, Lord God, Father all-powerful. Through Christ you created our world and keep it in existence; you give us the Spirit for our enlightenment and strength. For works of light you made the day, and for the refreshment of our minds and bodies you created the night. O loving Father, in your great compassion, accept our sacrifice of praise. As you have guided us safely through this year, grant us a grace-filled Lenten season that we might approach the day of your resurrection as renewed Christian people. We ask this Father, through your Son, Jesus and in the Holy Spirit; all praise and thanksgiving be yours, now and forever. Amen.

Psalms of Praise and Trust in God

Psalm 141

Leader:	I call to you, Lord; help me now!
People:	**I call to you, Lord; help me now!**
Leader:	Listen to me when I call to you. Receive my prayer as incense, my uplifted hands as an evening sacrifice.
People:	**I call to you, Lord; help me now!**
Leader:	Lord, place a guard at my mouth, a sentry at the door of my lips. Keep me from wanting to do wrong, or to join evil folks in their wickedness. May I never take part in their feasts!
People:	**I call to you, Lord; help me now!**
Leader:	A good man may punish me and reprimand me in kindness, but I will not let an evil man anoint my head, because I am always praying against his evil deeds.
People:	**When their rulers are thrown down on rocky cliffs, the people will admit that my words were true.**
Leader:	Like wood that is split and chopped into bits, so their bones are scattered at the edge of the grave.
People:	**But I, Lord God, keep trusting in you; I seek your protection; don't let me die!**
Leader:	Protect me from the traps they have set for me, from the snares of their evildoers. May the wicked fall into their own traps, while I go unharmed.
People:	**I call to you, Lord; help me now!**

Psalm-prayer

Minister:	Heavenly Father, we ask you to accept our prayer of repentance. Cleanse us of all that is sinful; renew our spirit that we may draw closer to you during this season of Lent. For this we pray, through Christ our Lord. Amen.

Psalm 27:1-4

Leader: The Lord is my light and my salvation; I will fear no one. The Lord protects me from all danger; I will not be afraid.

People: When evil men attack me and try to kill me, they stumble and fall. Even if a whole army surrounds me, I will not be afraid; even if my enemies attack me, I will still trust in God.

Leader: I have asked the Lord for one thing; one thing only do I want; to live in the Lord's house all my life, to marvel at his goodness, and to ask his guidance there.

People: Glory be to the Father, and to the Son and to the Holy Spirit, as it was in the beginning, is now, and ever shall be, world without end. Amen.

First Lesson   **Isaiah 6:1-8**

Reader 1: A reading from the prophet Isaiah. In the year that King Uzziah died I saw the Lord sitting upon a throne, high and lifted up; and his train filled the temple. Above him stood the seraphim; each had six wings; with two he covered his face, and with two he covered his feet, and with two he flew. And one called to another and said:

Reader 2: "Holy, holy, holy is the Lord of hosts; the whole earth is full of his glory."

Reader 1: And the foundations of the thresholds shook at the voice of him who called and the house was filled with smoke. And I said: "Woe is me! For I am lost; for I am a man of unclean lips, and I dwell in the midst of a people of unclean lips; for my eyes have seen the King, the Lord or hosts!"

Then flew one of the seraphim to me, having in his hand a burning coal which he had taken with tongs from the altar. And he touched my mouth, and said:

7

Reader 2: "Behold, this has touched your lips; your guilt is taken away, and your sin forgiven."

Reader 1: And I heard the voice of the Lord saying,

Reader 2: "Whom shall I send, and whom will go for us?"

Reader 1: Then I said, "Here am I! Send me!

(Time of silent reflection)

Gospel   **Matthew 3:13-17**

Reader: A reading from the Gospel of Matthew. At that time Jesus went from Galilee to the Jordan, and came to John to be baptized by him. But John tried to make him change his mind. "I ought to be baptized by you," John said, "yet you come to me! But Jesus answered him, "Let it be so for now. For in this way we shall do all that God requires." So John agreed. As soon as he was baptized, Jesus came up out of the water. Then heaven was opened to him, and he saw the Spirit of God coming down like a dove and lighting on him. And then a voice said from heaven, "This is my own dear Son, with whom I am well pleased." This is the Gospel of the Lord.

People: **Thanks be to God.**

Hymn of Praise

Sermon

New Testament Canticle   Revelation 11:17-18; 12:10b-12a

Leader: Lord God Almighty, who is and who was!

People: **We thank you that you have used your great power and have begun to rule!**

Leader: The heathen were filled with rage, because it is the time for your wrath to come, and for the dead to be judged.

8

People:	**It is the time to reward your servants, the prophets, and all your people, all who fear you, great and small alike.**
Leader:	Now God's salvation has come! Now God has shown his power as King! Now his Messiah has shown his authority! For the accuser of our brothers, who stood before God accusing them day and night, has been thrown out of heaven.
People:	**Our brothers won the victory over him by the blood of the Lamb, and by the truth which they proclaimed; and they were willing to give up their lives and die.**
Leader:	And so be glad, you heavens, and all you that live there!
People:	**Amen. Amen.**

Prayers of Intercession

People's response to each petition is **Lord, hear our prayer.**

Minister:	In the peace of the risen Christ, let us pray to the Lord.
Leader:	For this congregation and for all Christians during this time of Lent, let us pray to the Lord.
Leader:	For the leaders of our nation and leaders throughout the world, let us pray to the Lord.
Leader:	For peacemakers and those who work for social justice, let us pray to the Lord.
Leader:	For those who are sick and suffering, especially members of this congregation, let us pray to the Lord.
Leader:	For those who have died in the peace of Christ, let us pray to the Lord.
Minister:	Let us join in praying the words Jesus himself gave us. Our Father . . .

Imposition of Ashes

Those who wish may come forward to have the sign of the cross imposed on their foreheads.

9

Closing Benediction

Minister: May the blessing of God, Father, Son, and Holy Spirit, guide us throughout this week and always.

People: Amen.

(Take time to share a sign of peace.)

Closing Hymn

Service for Palm Sunday

Service of Celebration

The Prelude

The Call to Worship
Minister: Hosanna!
People: Hosanna to the Son of David!
Minister: Blessed is the King who comes in the name of the Lord!
People: Blessed be the kingdom of our father David that is coming!
Minister: Hosanna!
People: Hosanna in the highest!

The Hymn of Praise "Hosanna, Loud Hosanna"

The Collect
Father, on this day as we recall the entrance of our Savior into Jerusalem, grant that we may open our hearts and let him enter in and triumph within us anew. As we are mindful of the fact that he came not as a conqueror to destroy, but as a Messiah to save, we would praise you for the gift of salvation, through the same Jesus Christ our Lord. Amen.

The Gloria Patri

The Prayer of Confession
Forgive us, O Lord, wherein we have hailed you as our **Father one day and failed to acknowledge you twenty-four**

hours later; pardon us for calling ourselves your followers, yet denying you when the mood of our crowd changes; be merciful to us for desiring to be a member of your church, yet forsaking you when we are called upon to take a stand for our Christian convictions. Forgive us, O Lord, in the name of the One who gave his life for our sins and became our Savior. Amen.

The Assurance of Pardon

The Lord's Prayer

The Choral Selection

The Old Testament Scripture   Psalm 24:7-10 (RSV)
    Minister: Lift up your heads, O gates!
                And be lifted up, O ancient doors!
                That the King of glory may come in.
    People: **Who is the King of glory?**
                The Lord, strong and mighty,
                The Lord, mighty in battle!
    Minister: Lift up your heads, O gates!
                And be lifted up, O ancient doors!
                That the King of glory may come in!
    People: **Who is the King of glory?**
                The Lord of hosts,
                He is the King of glory!

The New Testatment Scripture   Matthew 21:1-11

The Hymn of Adoration   "All Glory, Laud, and Honor"

The Pastoral Prayer

The Dedication of Offerings

The Doxology

The Sermon

The Litany of Dedication
Minister: During this Holy Week, we will be tempted,
tried and tested in a manner similar to those
of old. May our faith be strengthened so that
he can depend upon us.
Will you fail him as Nicodemus did when he
refused to risk his position in the Sanhedrin?
People: **Lord, help me not to fail you.**
Minister: Will you be unconcerned about him as Herod
was when he failed to take a stand?
People: **Lord, help us to be concerned about you.**
Minister: Will you forsake him as Pilate did when he was
afraid to go against the wishes of the crowd?
People: **Lord, help us not to forsake you.**
Minister: Will you deny him as Peter did when he real-
ized his own life was in danger?
People: **Lord, help us not to deny you.**
Minister: Will you betray him as Judas did when he sold
him for thirty pieces of silver?
People: **Lord, help us not to betray you.**

The Prayer of Dedication

The Hymn of Faithfulness "Ride on, Ride on in Majesty"

The Benediction

The Postlude

13

Service for Maundy Thursday

Holy Communion Service

The Prelude

The Hymn of Praise

The Call to Worship

Minister: Christ revealed to us the new covenant which God promised to all who follow him.

People: It is a covenant written in our hearts instead of on tablets of stone.

Minister: It is a covenant with God, sealed by the blood of Christ, who died on the cross for our sins.

Minister: It is a new covenant in which we accept God's love and commit our lives to him.

All: We will thank God for this new covenant as we worship him in this hour together.

The Collect (In unison)

Almighty God, who promised a new covenant with your children, and who established that covenant through the death of your only Son; grant that we may so use this sacrament of bread and wine that the fruits of your redemption may continually be manifest in us, through Jesus Christ our Lord. Amen.

The Lord's Prayer

The Scripture Reading

The Covenant Litany

Minister: God made a covenant with Noah that the earth would never again be destroyed by a flood.

People: **We are thankful, O God, for your covenant.**

Minister: God made a covenant with Abraham that he would give the land of Canaan to him and his descendants.

People: **We are thankful, O God, for your covenant.**

Minister: God made a covenant with the children of Israel to be their God and to protect them.

People: **We are thankful, O God, for your covenant.**

Minister: God promised a new covenant, through the words of Jeremiah, for those who would follow him.

People: **We are thankful, O God, for your covenant.**

Minister: God sent Jesus to fulfill that covenant; he revealed the true mission of his life at the Last Supper.

People: **We are thankful, O God, that you sent your Son to reveal the fullness of this covenant, and the greatness of your love for us.**

The Covenant Prayer

The Offering and Doxology

The Hymn of Penitence

The Communion Meditation

The Invitation to the Sacrament

The Confesson of Sin (In unison)

Almighty God, we acknowledge that we have sinned against you in thought, word, and deed, and have not practiced your principle of love in our relationships with others. We earnestly repent of our sins, and are sorry for all of our transgressions. Our hearts are filled with guilt, and while we know that we do not deserve your goodness, we ask you to grant us your pardon. Cleanse our spirits from within, O Lord, and guide us that we might live a renewed and righteous life after the example of Jesus Christ, in whose name we pray. Amen.

The Assurance of Pardon

The Prayer of Confession (In unison)
Almight God, as we are met here to partake of this bread and wine, we pray that we might yield our hearts to your Spirit. We commemorate the Last Supper of Jesus with his disciples, and the offering of himself upon the cross. We pray that you would sanctify these elements of bread and wine, which we now consecrate to their sacred use, representing for us the body that was broken and the blood that was shed on our behalf. As we receive this sacrament, we pray that we might be renewed in spirit, and that we might be faithful disciples, following the example of Jesus; in his name. Amen.

The Words of Institution

The Serving of the Sacrament

The Prayer of Thanksgiving (In unison)
Eternal God, we most heartily thank you that we have been strengthened in spirit through this holy sacrament. We have also been drawn nearer to all other Christians through our common belief and practice. We rejoice with them, knowing that we have all become heirs of your eternal kingdom by the merits of the death of your beloved Son. So guide us, Lord, by the grace of your Holy Spirit, that we may live according to your will, through Jesus Christ our Lord, Amen.

The Hymn of Consecration

The Benediction

The Postlude

Service for Good Friday

Friday of Holy Week

Opening Hymn   "O Sacred Head Now Wounded"
                          "When I Survey the Wondrous Cross"

Call To Worship
    Minister: Come let us worshp the God who has called
                us together this day and every day to be his
                people.
    People: **May God open our mouths to proclaim his**
                praise this day.
    Minister: Come, let us acclaim the God of our salvation,
                whose son Jesus died that we might live.
    People: **May God open our hearts to such a gift of love.**
    Minister: Father, today we ponder a great mystery of our
                faith — the death of your son, Jesus. Today
                we also reflect upon our own daily dying to self
                and the challenge that it brings. Help us to look
                at the cross and be encouraged and strength-
                ened to meet a new day. This we ask through
                Jesus your son. Amen.

Litany of Confession
    Leader: For the times we have given in to despair, ig-
                noring the promise of your continued love for
                us, we pray: Lord, have mercy.
    People: **Lord have mercy.**

19

Leader:	For the times we have turned our faces from those in need, preferring instead the comforts of the good life, we pray: Christ have mercy.
People:	**Christ have mercy.**
Leader:	For the times we have failed to accept the challenge of the cross in our daily lives, we pray: Lord have mercy.
People:	**Lord have mercy.**
Minister:	Father, we acknowledge our failings as a Christian people and ask you to strengthen our commitment. May the great mysteries of our faith, encountered during this Lenten season, renew us in your service, This we ask through Jesus. Amen.

First Lesson   **Isaiah 53:3-7**

Responsive Psalm   **Psalm 40:1-5**

Leader:	We waited patiently for the Lord's help; then he listened to us and heard our cry.
People:	**He pulled us out of a dangerous pit, out of the deadly quicksand. He set us safely on a rock and made us secure.**
Leader:	He taught us to sing a new song a song of praise to our God. Many who see this will take warning and will put their trust in the Lord.
People:	**Happy are those who trust the Lord, who do not turn to idols or join those who worship false gods.**
Leader:	You have done many things for us, O Lord our God; there is no one like you.
People:	**You have made many wonderful plans for us. We could never speak of them all — their number is so great.**

Gospel   **John 19:17-30**

Narrator: So they took charge of Jesus. He went out, carrying his cross, and came to "The Place of the Skull," as it is called. (In Hebrew it is called "Golgotha.") There they crucified him; and they also crucified two other men, one on each side, with Jesus between them. Pilate wrote a notice, and had it put on the cross: "Jesus of Nazareth, the King of the Jews." Many people read it, because the place where Jesus was crucified was not far from the city. The notice was written in Hebrew, Latin, and Greek. The chief priests said to Pilate,

Reader 1: Do not write "The King of the Jews," but rather, "This man said, 'I am the King of the Jews.' "

Narrator: Pilate answered them,

Reader 2: "What I have written stays written."

Narrator: After the soldiers had crucified Jesus, they took his clothes and divided them into four parts, one part for each soldier. They also took the robe, which ws made of one piece of woven cloth without any seams in it. The soldiers said to one another,

Reader: "Let's not tear it; let's throw dice to see who will get it."

Narrator: This happened in order to make the scripture come true which said: "They divided my clothes among themselves and gambled for my robe." Standing close to Jesus' cross were his mother, his mother's sister, Mary the wife of Clopas, and Mary Magdalene. Jesus saw his mother and the disciple he loved standing there; so he said to his mother,

Jesus: "He is your son."

Narrator: Then he said to the disciple,

Jesus: "She is your mother."

Narrator:	From that time on the disciple took her to live in his home. Jesus knew that by now everything had been completed; and in order to make the scripture come true, he said,
Jesus:	"I am thirsty."
Narrator:	A bowl was there, full of cheap wine; so a sponge was soaked in the wine, put on a stalk of hyssop, and lifted to up to his lips. Jesus drank the wine and said,
Jesus:	"It is finished."
Narrator:	Then he bowed his head and died.

Hymn   "Jesus, Keep Me Near the Cross"
"Were You There When They Crucified My Lord"

Sermon

Prayers of Intercession

Minister:	Let us bring our needs to the Father at this time, that, as a community, we might share our hopes and dreams with one another.
Leader:	For our nation's leaders, as they attempt to provide moral and political leadership during ever-challenging times.
People:	**Lord, hear our prayer.**
Leader:	For peace throughout the world, especially in those countries most torn by war.
People:	**Lord, hear our prayer.**
Leader:	For the poor, the sick, the despairing within this local community.
People:	**Lord, hear our prayer.**
Leader:	For our Christian community, gathered here this day, that it might grow in the hope and love of Christ.
People:	**Lord, hear our prayer.**
Leader:	PLease mention your own special needs at this time, silently or aloud, as you wish.

(Time for spontaneous prayer.)

Minister: We look to Christ for the courage to face the many human no's of our daily life. We also look to one another for encouragement and support as we attempt to speak our own resounding yes to the challenge of the Gospel. Let us take a moment now to share Christ's hope and peace with those around us. May the peace of the Lord be always with you.

People: **And also with you.**

(Sharing a Sign of Peace.)

A Hymn of Hope "O God Our Help in Ages Past"
"Peace, to Soothe Our Bitter Woes"
"I Know That My Redeemer Lives"

Minister: Gathering our needs into one, let us pray now with the words of Jesus himself. Our Father . . .

Benediction

Minister: Let us bow our heads now and pray for God's blessing. Lord, bless and strengthen your people in their service of you.

People: **Amen.**

Minister: Lord, give your people the courage to say "yes" to life's challenges.

People: **Amen.**

Minister: May the blessing of God, Father, Son, and Holy Spirit be with you this day and forever. Amen.

Closing Hymn "Be Thou My Vision"
"The King of Love My Shepherd Is"
"Amazing Grace, How Sweet the Sound"

---

*Several hymns which capture the theme of the service have been suggested at various points throughout; from them, or your own repertoire, a choice of one hymn may be made.

23

Service for Good Friday

The Nails of the Cross

The Prelude

The Hymn

The Call to Worship

Minister: Surely he has borne our griefs and carried our sorrows; yet we did esteem him stricken, smitten of God, and afflicted.

People: **But he was wounded for our transgressions, he was bruised for our iniquities, the chastisement of our peace was upon him; and with his stripes we are healed.**

Minister: For our sake he made him to be sin who knew no sin, so that we might become the righteousness of God.

People: **In him we have redemption through his blood, the forgiveness of our trespasses, according to the riches of his grace which he lavished upon us.**

The Collect (In unison)

O merciful God, who did not spare your only Son, but delivered him up for us all, that he might bear our sins upon the cross; grant that we might so examine ourselves that we realize our own sinfulness, so great as to spiritually crucify him anew. Help us to recognize those nails which we drive into his cross today, as we ask you to transform us into faithful disciples, in his name. Amen.

The Nail of Pride

The Scripture Reading   **Mark 12:38-40**

The Meditation

The Prayer (In Unison)
Almighty God, in this hour of solemn remembrance we acknowledge with horror and shame that we have sinned against you in many ways. We know that we have thought more highly or ourselves than we ought, and that our pride has been evident in our haughty spirits. Forgive us of our hypocrisy and help us to learn the lesson of humility, through Christ our Lord. Amen.

The Silent Moments of Reflection

The Hymn

The Nail of Betrayal

The Scripture Reading   **Matthew 26:47-56**

The Meditation

The Prayer (In Unison)
Gracious God, we are shocked by the betrayal of Judas, and yet we fail to realize the ways in which we deny our Savior today. We have followed the crowd and have done the will of the majority, without considering whether our decisions were Christian. Forgive us for failing to stand up for those principles he taught, as in his name we pray. Amen.

The Silent Moments of Reflection

The Hymn

26

The Nail of Envy

The Scripture Reading   Matthew 27:15-18

The Meditation

The Prayer (In unison)
Merciful God, we ask you to pardon us for being envious
of others; those who succeed where we have failed, those
who prosper while we have financial problems, those who
have excellent health while we are in pain, those who receive
special favors while we are rejected. Help us to realize that
you love each one of us, as we pray in the name of the one
who died for us. Amen.

The Silent Moments of Reflection

The Hymn

The Nail of Indecision

The Scripture Reading   Matthew 27:20-26

The Meditation

The Prayer (In unison)
Eternal God, we know that we have had a lukewarm faith,
and have failed to make the Christian decision many times.
We have also made the wrong decision by waiting too long
to make any decision, while others made it for us. Forgive
us, we pray, and help us to be firm in our faith and to make
decisions which are consistent with the principles of Christ;
in Jesus' name. Amen.

The Silent Moments of Reflection

The Hymn

The Nail of Hatred

The Scripture Reading   Luke 6:22, 32-35

The Meditation

The Prayer (In unison)
> God of Love, our hearts have been filled with anger and resentment, and we have expressed this to those around us. We have rejected those who were not like us and have not tried to love them. Forgive us, and help us to see beyond our own selfishness. Fill our hearts with love, and guide us in expressing this love to others, in the name of Jesus, our Savior. Amen.

The Silent Moments of Reflection

The Hymn

The Nail of Cruelty

The Scripture Reading

The Meditation

The Prayer (In unison)
> Almighty God, forgive us of the sin of cruelty, as well as the other sins that have driven spiritual nails into the cross of Christ. And now, we offer and present ourselves to you, that our souls and bodies might be reasonable, holy, and living sacrifices. Accept us as we are, and make us fit for service in your Church and in your kingdom. This we ask in the name of Jesus Christ, our Lord. Amen.

The Silent Moments of Reflection

The Hymn

The Benediction

The Postlude

Service
for
Easter

Sunrise Service

Opening Hymn

Call to Worship   **Psalm 96**

Minister: Sing a new song to the Lord!
Sing to the Lord, all the world!

**People: Sing to the Lord, and praise him!
Proclaim every day the good news that he has
saved us.**

Minister: Proclaim his glory to the nations, his mighty
acts to all peoples.

**People: Praise the Lord, all people on earth;
praise his glory and might.**

Minister: Praise the Lord's glorious name;
bring an offering and come into his Temple.

**People: Bow down before the Holy One when he ap-
pears; tremble before him, all the earth!**

Minister: Sing a new song to the Lord!
Sing to the Lord, all the world!

**People: Sing to the Lord, and praise him!
Proclaim every day the good news that he has
saved us.**

Minister: God, our Father, through the resurrection of
Jesus, your Son, you conquered the power of
sin and death and thus gave us new hope. Fill
us today with your Spirit that our celebration
might renew us in the living of the Christian
life. We ask this through Jesus your Son and
the Holy Spirit, one God, forever and ever.

People: Amen.

First Lesson   **Acts 10:34-43**

Minister: Today's First Lesson is a portion of the speech
              given by the Apostle Peter in the home of Cor-
              nelius. It was not unusual for Peter to be giv-
              ing sermons and speeches; however, it was
              unusual for Peter to be preaching about Jesus
              in the home of a Gentile — a non-Jewish per-
              son. Cornelius was a captain in the Roman
              army. He was a religious man but he was not
              a Jew. One day Cornelius had a vision. A man
              in shining clothes told him that God was
              pleased with him, and that he should send for
              a man named Peter. And so Peter came to visit
              Cornelius; this is part of what he had to say
              to Cornelius and his family.

Reader: Acts 10:34-43
              Peter began to speak: "I now realize that it is
              true that God treats everyone on the same ba-
              sis. Whoever fears him and does what is right
              is acceptable to him, no matter what race he
              belongs to. You know the message he sent to
              the people of Israel, proclaiming the Good
              News of peace through Jesus Christ, who is
              Lord of all. You know of the great event that
              took place throughout the land of Israel, be-
              ginning in Galilee after John preached his mes-
              sage of baptism. You know about Jesus of
              Nazareth and how God poured out on him the
              Holy Spirit and power. He went everywhere,
              doing good and healing all who were under the
              power of the Devil, for God was with him. We
              are witnesses of everything that he did in the
              land of Israel and in Jerusalem. Then they put
              him to death by nailing him to a cross. But God
              raised him up from death three days later and
              caused him to appear, not to everyone, but only
              to the witnesses that God had already chosen,

30

that is, to us who ate and drank with him after he rose from death. And he commanded us to preach the gospel to the people and to testify that he is the one whom God has appointed judge of the living and the dead. All the prophets spoke about him, saying that everyone who believes in him will have his sins forgiven through the power of his name.''

Second Lesson   **Colossians 3:1-4**
Reader 1: Today's Second Lesson is taken from Paul's letter to the Colossians. It is a short passage which reflects on the resurrection of Jesus and the effect of that event on his followers.
Reader 2: You have been raised to life with Christ, so set your hearts on the things that are in heaven, where Christ sits on his throne at the right side of God. Keep your minds fixed on the things there, not on things here on earth. For you have died, and your life is hidden with Christ in God. You real life is Christ and when he appears, then you too will appear with him and share his glory!

Gospel   **John 20:1-18**
(Choose a family — mother, father, and teen-age son — to proclaim the Gospel.)
Father: Early on Sunday morning, while it was still dark, Mary Magdalene went to the tomb and saw that the stone had been taken away from the entrance. She went running to Simon Peter and the other disciples, whom Jesus loved, and told them:
Mother: "They have taken the Lord from the tomb, and we don't know where they have put him!"
Father: Then Peter and the other disciple went to the tomb. The two of them were running, but the other disciple ran faster than Peter and reached the tomb first. He bent over and saw the

linen cloths, but he did not go in. Behind came Simon Peter, and he went straight into the tomb. He saw the linen cloths lying there and the cloth which had been around Jesus' head. It was not lying with the linen cloths but was rolled up by itself. Then the other disciple, who had reached the tomb first, also went in; he saw and believed. (They still did not understand the scripture which said that he must rise from death.) Then the disciples went back home. Mary stood crying outside the tomb. While she was still crying, she bent over and looked in the tomb and saw two angels there dressed in white, sitting where the body of Jesus had been, one at the head and the other at the feet. They asked her:

Son:	"Woman why are you crying?"
Father:	She answered:
Mother:	"They have taken my Lord away, and I do not know where they have put him!"
Father:	Then she turned around and saw Jesus standing there; but she did not know that it was Jesus. He asked her:
Son:	"Woman, why are you crying? Who is it that you are looking for?"
Father:	She thought he was the gardener, so she said to him:
Mother:	"If you took him away, sir, tell me where you have put him, and I will go and get him."
Father:	Jesus said to her:
Son:	"Mary!"
Father:	She turned to him and said in Hebrew:
Mother:	"Rabboni!"
Father:	This means "teacher." Jesus said to her:
Son:	"Do not hold on to me because I have not yet gone back up to the Father. But go to my brothers and tell them that I am returning to

him who is my Father and their Father, my God and their God.''

Father: So Mary Magdalene went and told the disciples that she had seen the Lord and related to them what he had told her. This is the Good News of Jesus the Lord!

Hymn

(Have a family bring flowers and a white cloth to be placed on and around the cross.)

Sermon

Offering

**A Prayer of Thanks
for the Victory of the Cross**   **Psalm 118**

Leader: Give thanks to the Lord, because he is good and his love is eternal.

People: Give thanks to the Lord, because he is good and his love is eternal.

Leader: Let the people of Israel say, ''His love is eternal.''

People: His power has brought us victory — his mighty power in battle!

Leader: I will not die; instead, I will live and proclaim what the Lord has done.

People: The stone which the builders rejected as worthless turned out to be the most important of all.

Leader: This was done by the Lord; what a wonderful sight it is!

People: This is the day of the Lord's victory; let us be happy, let us celebrate!

Leader: Give thanks to the Lord because he is good

People: and his love is eternal.

Hymn of Praise

The Lord's Prayer

33

Sharing of the Peace

Closing Benediction

Minister: Bow your heads and prayer for God's blessing. Through the resurrection of Jesus, God has
made you his children. May you be filled with
joy.

People: **Amen.**

Minister: You have been redeemed and set free. May you
live as people of hope.

People: **Amen.**

Minister: Your faith has allowed you to rise with him in
baptism. May you live holy and Spirit-filled
lives.

People: **Amen.**

Minister: May God bless you, the Father, and the Son,
and the Holy Spirit.

People: **Amen.**

Preparation for Worship

1. Large cross should be placed in prominent position.
2. Select a family who will drape the cross with a white cloth
and place flowers around it at the appropriate time during
the service.
3. Select a family to proclaim the Gospel.

Service
for
Easter

Easter Morning Service

The Prelude

The Call to Worship

Leader: "Christ has been raised from the dead, and become the first fruits of those who have fallen asleep." (1 Corinthians 15:20)

People: Christ is risen!

Leader: "Christ being raised from the dead will never die again; death no longer has dominion over him." (Romans 6:9)

People: Christ is risen!

Leader: Jesus said, "I am the resurrection and the life; he who believes in me, though he die, yet shall he live, and whoever lives and believes in me shall never die." (John 11:25, 26)

People: Christ is risen!

Leader: Our Lord said, "I am the first and the last, the living one; I died, and behold I am alive for evermore." (Revelation 1:17, 18)

People: Christ is risen!
He is risen indeed!

The Hymn of Praise

The Collect

Almighty God, who through the death of your Son overcame death, and through his resurrection have brought to us newness of life and immortality: grant that we may be able to see beyond the darkness of our cares and problems, and find new life within. Send your Spirit to roll away the stones from our hearts, that we may believe, even if we haven't seen. Help us to walk into the unknown future by faith, and not by sight, to trust and not be afraid. Continue to bless us, and strengthen us by your Spirit, as we share together in the wonder and glory of this day, through Christ our Lord. Amen.

The Litany of New Life

Leader: We worship in the glory of the light of a new day, having left the darkness of yesterday behind.

People: We thank you, O God, for changing darkness to light.

Leader: We know that we have been changed from sinners into followers of Christ, through his death upon the cross.

People: We thank you, O God, for saving us from our sins.

Leader: We see the trees and flowers, having lost their leaves and petals, now springing forth into the beauty of blossoms again.

People: We thank you, O God, for bringing forth new life around us.

Leader: We are aware of the manner in which the dingy caterpillar has been transformed into the beauty of the butterfly.

People: We thank you, O God, for transforming life before us.

Leader: We are reminded of the suffering and death of Jesus, and how he came forth again in a glorified, resurrected body.

People: We thank you, O God, for the glory of the resurrection.

Leader: We know that someday we shall die and leave
           this world, only to rise anew in the joy of eter-
           nal life.

People: **We thank you, O God, for the joy of eternal
           life.**

The Choral Selection

The Scripture Reading

The Call to Prayer
Leader: Bring us hope in the midst of our defeat, O Ris-
           en Lord, as we seek out your presence through
           prayer.

People: **Comfort us in our sadness, O Risen Lord, as
           we are reminded anew of your promise of eter-
           nal life.**

Leader: Guide us with the light of your spiritual
           presence, O Risen Lord, as we walk through
           the darkness of this world.

People: **Help us to have a stronger faith, O Risen Lord,
           as we seek to rise from the depths of despair
           to the heights of a newer, greater life.**

The Easter Prayer

The Presentation of the Easter Offering

The Doxology

The Hymn of Triumph

The Easter Meditation

The Challenge of Christian Witness
Leader: Go forth and tell everyone that Christ is risen!

People: **We will tell them that he triumphed over death
           and the grave.**

Leader: Tell them that his spirit is alive in the world today.

People: **We will praise him with our words and our deeds. Alleluia!**

The Hymn of Joy

The Benediction

The Postlude

www.ingramcontent.com/pod-product-compliance
Lightning Source LLC
Chambersburg PA
CBHW071759020426
42331CB00008B/2319